THE WORLD'S

FOOD RESOURCES

Robin Kerrod

Thomson Learning
New York

First published in the United States in 1994 by
Thomson Learning, 115 Fifth Avenue, New York, NY 10003

First published in 1993 by Wayland (Publishers) Ltd.

Library of Congress Cataloging-in-Publication Data
Kerrod, Robin.
Food resources / Robin Kerrod.
p. cm. (The World's resources)
Includes bibliographical references (p.) and index.
ISBN 1-56847-108-4 : $14.95
1. Agriculture — Juvenile literature. 2. Food supply — Juvenile literature. 3. Food crops — Juvenile literature. 4. Livestock — Juvenile literature. 5. Fisheries — Juvenile literature. [1. Food supply. 2. Food crops. 3. Domestic animals. 4. Fisheries.]
I. Title. II. Series.
S519.K43 1994
338.1'9 — dc20 93-34612

Designed and illustrated by Talkback International Ltd., London
Printed in Italy

Other books in the series
Energy Resources
Material Resources
Mineral Resources

Cover pictures (top to bottom): Combine harvester, rice paddy, commercial fishing, map of dairy farming areas in Switzerland.

The Maps

This book contains two kinds of maps: world maps like the one below and area maps, which show only parts of the world. The map below will help you to locate the regions shown in the area maps. Each of the red boxes on this map outlines one of the regions shown in the book. Each box also contains the number of the page on which you can find detailed information about that region.

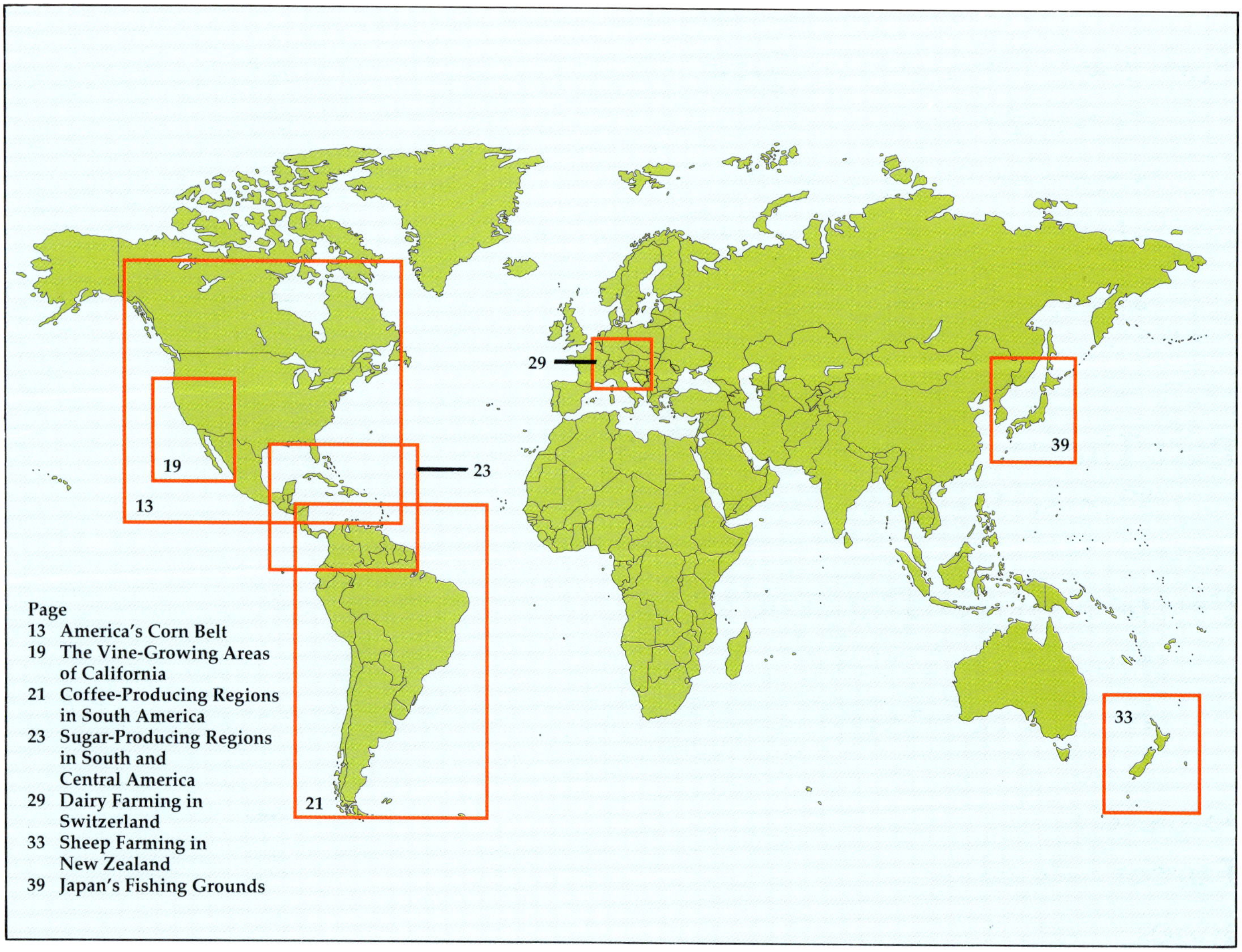

CONTENTS

Introduction

Farmers feed the world. They grow crops and raise livestock to produce food for themselves and for the rest of the population. Farming, or agriculture, is the world's most important industry.

The amount of land available for farming is limited. Only about one-ninth of the earth's surface is suitable for growing crops, and a slightly larger area is suitable for grazing livestock. The remainder is covered by mountains, forests, deserts, and ice.

Our earliest ancestors were not farmers. They wandered from place to place looking for their food in the wild. They gathered the edible parts of wild plants. For meat, they hunted animals and ate small creatures such as grubs and lizards.

About 14,000 years ago, people began to domesticate (tame) wild animals and raise them for food. About 10,000 years ago, people began growing their own crops, particularly cereals. To do this, they had to settle in permanent villages, which led to the first civilizations in the Middle East. Some scholars believe that the first farmers were women: the women tended crops while the men hunted.

At first, farmers cultivated their crops by hand. Later they began to use the ox-drawn plow. In this way they were able to cultivate more land and increase crop production. The introduction of farm machinery during the eighteenth and nineteenth centuries led to even greater productivity. Today, machines dominate farming in some parts of the world, although in developing countries much farm work is still done by hand.

Every year, the world's population increases, which means that more food is needed. The widespread use of machines is one of the reasons farming has been able to keep pace with increasing food demand. Other scientific advancements have also helped to increase the quantity of crops and livestock.

▶ A Pakistani vegetable-seller displays his produce by the roadside.

PART ONE

Farm Crops

▼ This picture shows familiar foods from six groups. It was thought that for a balanced diet people should eat at least one item from each group at every meal. Now some health practitioners argue that people should eat more grains and vegetables and less meat and dairy products.

Thousands of plants produce seeds, fruits, leaves, stems, and roots that we can eat. However, only about 50 of these plants are widely grown as farm crops. Farmers must choose crops that will grow well in the local climate and soil.

By far the most important crops are cereals, which provide grain. The main cereals are wheat, corn, and rice. Together, they supply about half the world's nourishment. Other major cereals include barley, sorghum, and millet. All cereals are members of the grass family and produce seeds as heads of grain.

The Elements of a Balanced Diet

▲ This medieval illustration shows people cultivating crops by hand.

Basic foods

Almost half of all farmland in the world is devoted to cereals. They are staple crops, which means that they provide a basic diet for the population. Cereals are rich in carbohydrates, which provide energy for the body, and proteins, which the body needs for muscles, bones, and other tissues to grow.

Vegetables and fruits also form part of a healthy diet. In some countries, vegetables are the staple crop. Potatoes grow well in cool

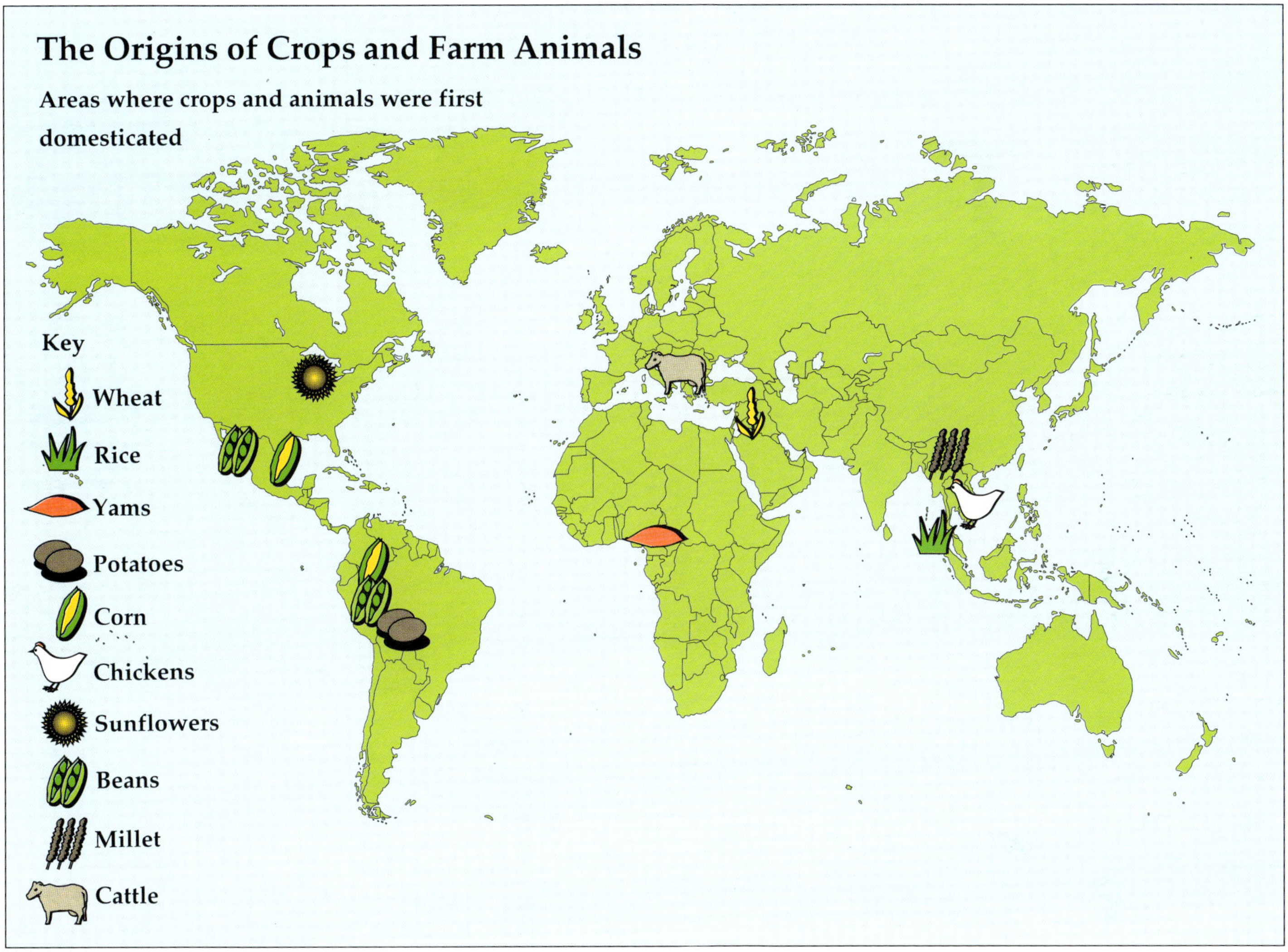

climates and cassava in warm ones. In some regions legumes, such as beans, are staples. Among other major crops are the beverage crops, such as tea and coffee.

Sugar comes from sugarcane and sugar beet, and vegetable oils come from such crops as olives and sunflower seeds.

Crops versus livestock

Crop farming in general makes much better use of the land than livestock farming. For example, a field that is sown with wheat produces about three tons per acre every year. If the same field were grazed by dairy cattle, they would produce about four tons of milk per acre. However, wheat contains about three times the carbohydrate and about twice the protein of milk. If the field were used to raise beef cattle, it would produce even less food per acre. Growing grains is the most efficient use of farmland.

Growing Crops

The amount of land available for growing crops is limited, yet the population is always increasing. As a result farmers have found ways to increase the productivity of the land. They have learned to select the right crops for their land and to prepare the land well before sowing. They have also learned the value of fertilizers, which put back into the soil the nourishing minerals and other substances that growing crops take out. Farmers also know that they must protect crops against diseases, pests, and weeds.

▲ Some farmers use airplanes to dust crops with chemical fertilizers.

Over the past few decades, crop yields (the amount of a crop produced by the available land) throughout the world have increased very rapidly as a result of the "Green Revolution." This revolution in agriculture was brought about by the introduction of new crop varieties and the widespread use of chemicals to make the soil more productive and to protect the crops from disease and insect pests.

SLASH AND BURN

In many developing countries in the tropics, people are still using the traditional "slash-and-burn" method of clearing forest land for farming. They cut down the trees and burn the wood. The land is fertile for just a few years and then the crops begin to fail. The farmers then clear another patch of forest, leaving the poor land behind. If the land is left undisturbed, it might eventually return to forest, but this could take many years.

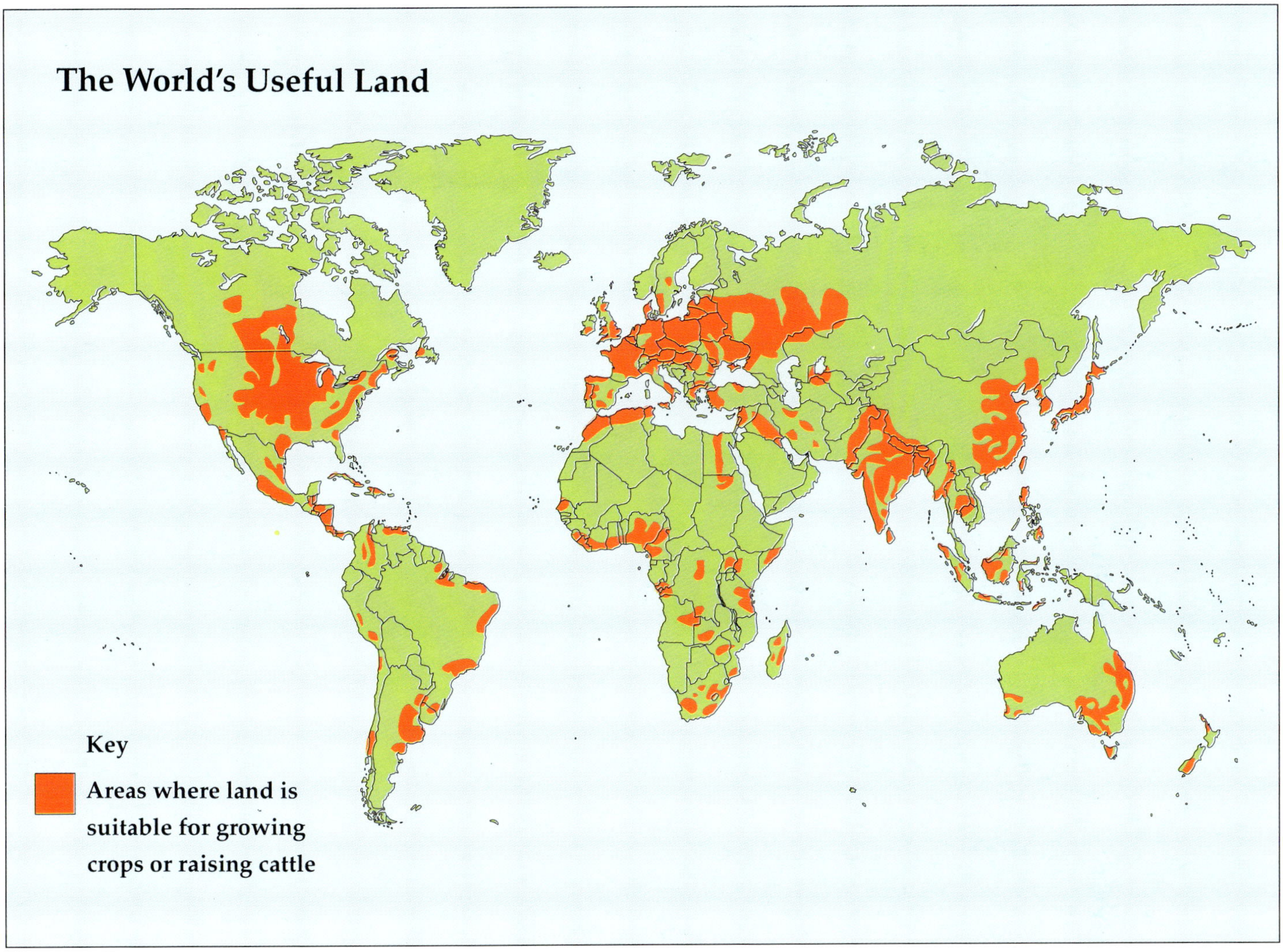

Agricultural chemicals

One of the chemicals most widely used for fertilizing the soil is superphosphate, which is produced from phosphate rock. Chemicals called ammonium and potassium nitrates are also used as fertilizers. On a smaller scale, animal dung and processed human sewage are used as fertilizers, especially in countries where farmers cannot afford to buy expensive chemical fertilizers.

Insects, fungus diseases, and weeds can attack crops or keep them from growing properly. Treating crops with the appropriate chemicals – pesticides, fungicides, and herbicides – can combat all these threats. However, they can also have a harmful effect on the environment (see page 40). Many farmers who can afford to use such chemicals have chosen not to.

Crop Cultivation

Each crop needs tending, or cultivating, in a different way. But some parts of the process of cultivation are similar for many crops. The ground is prepared to receive seeds or young plants, followed by sowing the seeds or planting. While growing, the crop needs to be watered and weeded; it may also need to be sprayed with chemicals. When the crop is mature, it must be picked.

In developed countries, crops are cultivated by a few workers using machines. In less developed countries, large numbers of workers do the work by hand.

Wheat is the world's most important crop and provides a good example of the way many crops are cultivated.

▼ In the developed countries of the world, farm equipment such as the combine harvester is a familiar sight.

▼ This graph shows the percentage of the work force who are farmers. Less developed countries such as Nepal need to employ more laborers than developed countries, which can afford machines to help with the hard work.

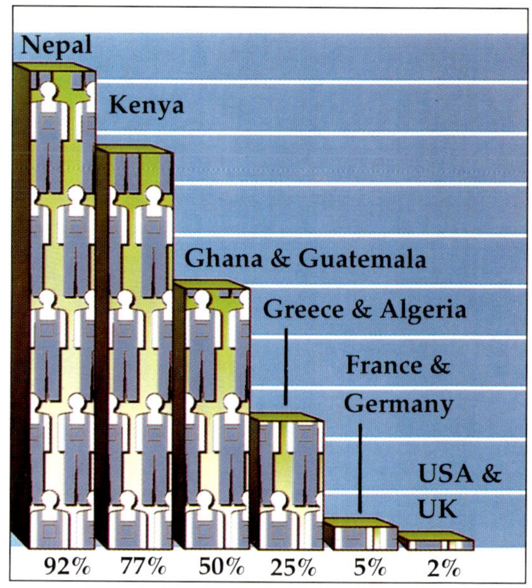

Plowing and drilling

Plowing is the first stage in preparing the soil for sowing. The blades of the plow cut into the ground and turn over slices of soil. This buries weeds and makes a distinctive pattern in the soil.

Next comes harrowing, a kind of raking process done with frames carrying spikes or disks. It levels

the surface and breaks up clods in the soil so it will be ready to receive the seed.

Sowing takes place in autumn or spring. A seed drill is used to place the wheat seeds beneath the surface in straight lines and at the right depth. Fertilizer is usually applied at the same time.

Harvesting

As the wheat grows, it is sprayed several times with chemicals to keep weeds, insects, and plant diseases at bay. In summer, the wheat "ears" (heads of grain) ripen and turn golden brown.

The crop is now ready for harvesting by a combine harvester. This machine combines the actions of reaping (cutting the wheat) and threshing (separating the grain). The largest combine harvesters can cut a strip over ten yards wide and can harvest up to ten acres of wheat per hour.

Wheat and Corn

More wheat is grown in the world than any other crop: about 660 million tons are produced every year. Wheat provides a staple food for one-third of the world's people.

Wheat is used mainly to make flour, which in turn is made into bread and pasta. Wheat is good for making bread because it contains a substance called gluten, which gives bread its spongy texture. A lot of wheat is also fed to livestock.

Wheat grows best in climates that are neither too hot nor too cold and have reasonable rainfall. Among the biggest wheat-growing regions are the vast prairies of the United States and Canada and the steppe regions of southern Russia and the Ukraine. The prairies and steppes are each capable of producing 110 million tons of wheat per year. The wheat fields of China also produce nearly this much.

▲ Farm workers in Peru harvest corn by hand.

Other wheat-like grains that are widely grown include barley and rye, which can be distinguished from wheat by their "whiskered" grain. Some 200 million tons of barley are grown each year, and it is largely used in brewing and as food for livestock.

▶ Grain is unloaded into a barn for drying.

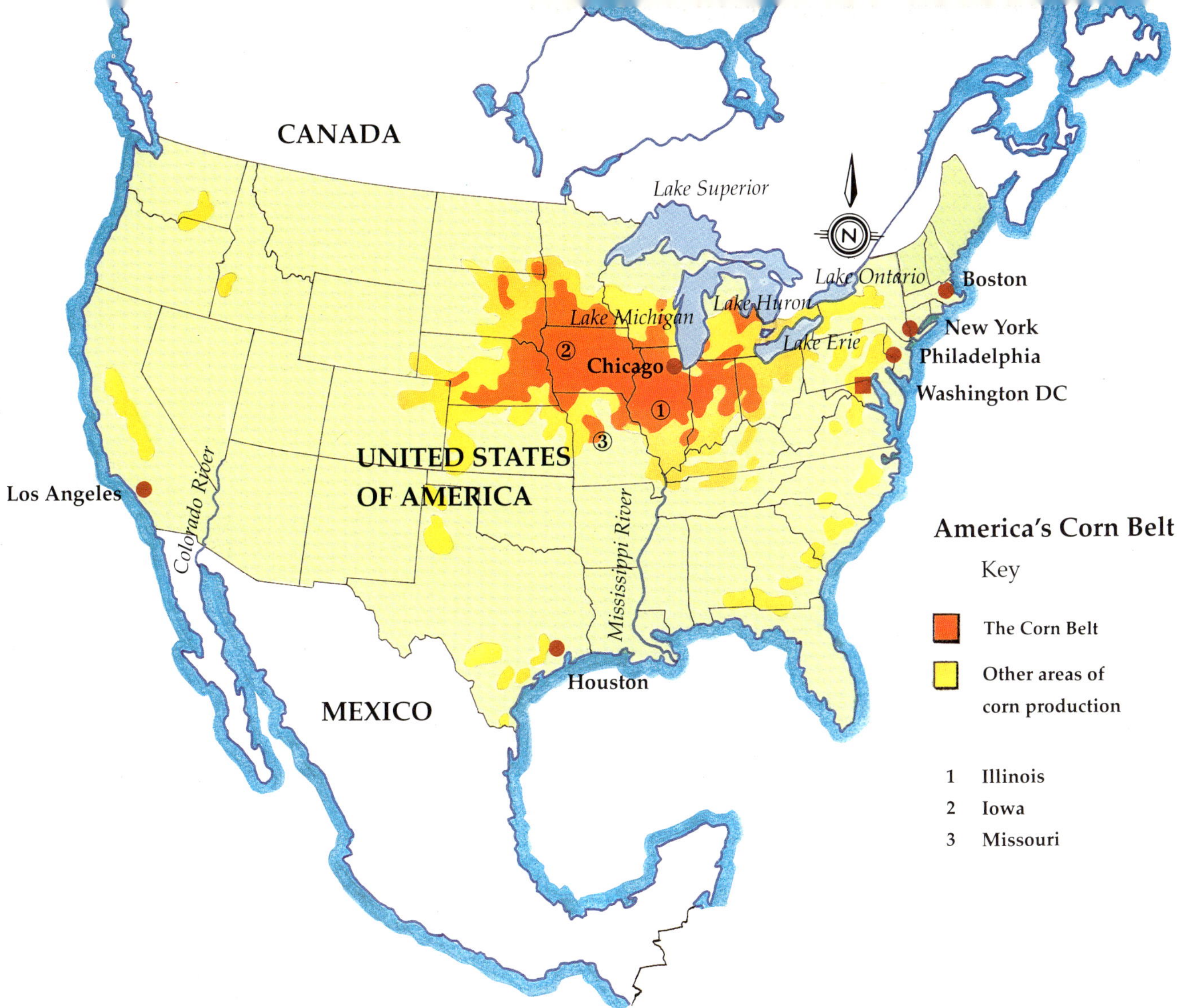

Corn

Corn, which is also called maize, is cultivated in much the same way as wheat, but grows best in a warmer climate. Unlike other grains, corn produces its grain in large cobs, which grow from a thick stem. Each cob is made up of several hundred grains.

Some 525 million tons of corn are produced every year, making it the world's third most important grain, after wheat and rice. Corn originally came from the Americas, and it is now produced in the largest quantities by the United States (more than 220 million tons a year). The most productive region is centered in Illinois, Iowa, and Missouri. This area is known as the Corn Belt.

In the United States and Europe, most corn is fed to livestock. In parts of South America and Africa, however, it is a staple food for people. Familiar products of corn include corn-on-the-cob, popcorn, cornstarch, corn oil, and breakfast foods, including muffins and cereal.

Rice

Rice is the world's second most important cereal crop. For millions of people in southern and southeast Asia, the daily meal consists of rice and a few vegetables. Rice is usually eaten as grain; it is also made into breakfast foods, rice cakes, and flour. The largest quantities of rice are grown in China and India. China produces about 200 million tons a year, out of the world total of about 565 million tons.

Rice is a semitropical plant that grows best in regions that remain warm and wet all year. It is farmed there by a system of wet cultivation, which has scarcely changed for centuries. Some rice is also cultivated in the warm temperate regions of the U.S., South America, and Australia. In these places, rice is often grown in much the same way as wheat, on dry land.

Rice is usually grown in flooded fields, called paddies, which are drained when the rice ripens. Because paddies need a constant supply of water, they are often found in river valleys. Paddies are

▼ Rice growing in paddies in China

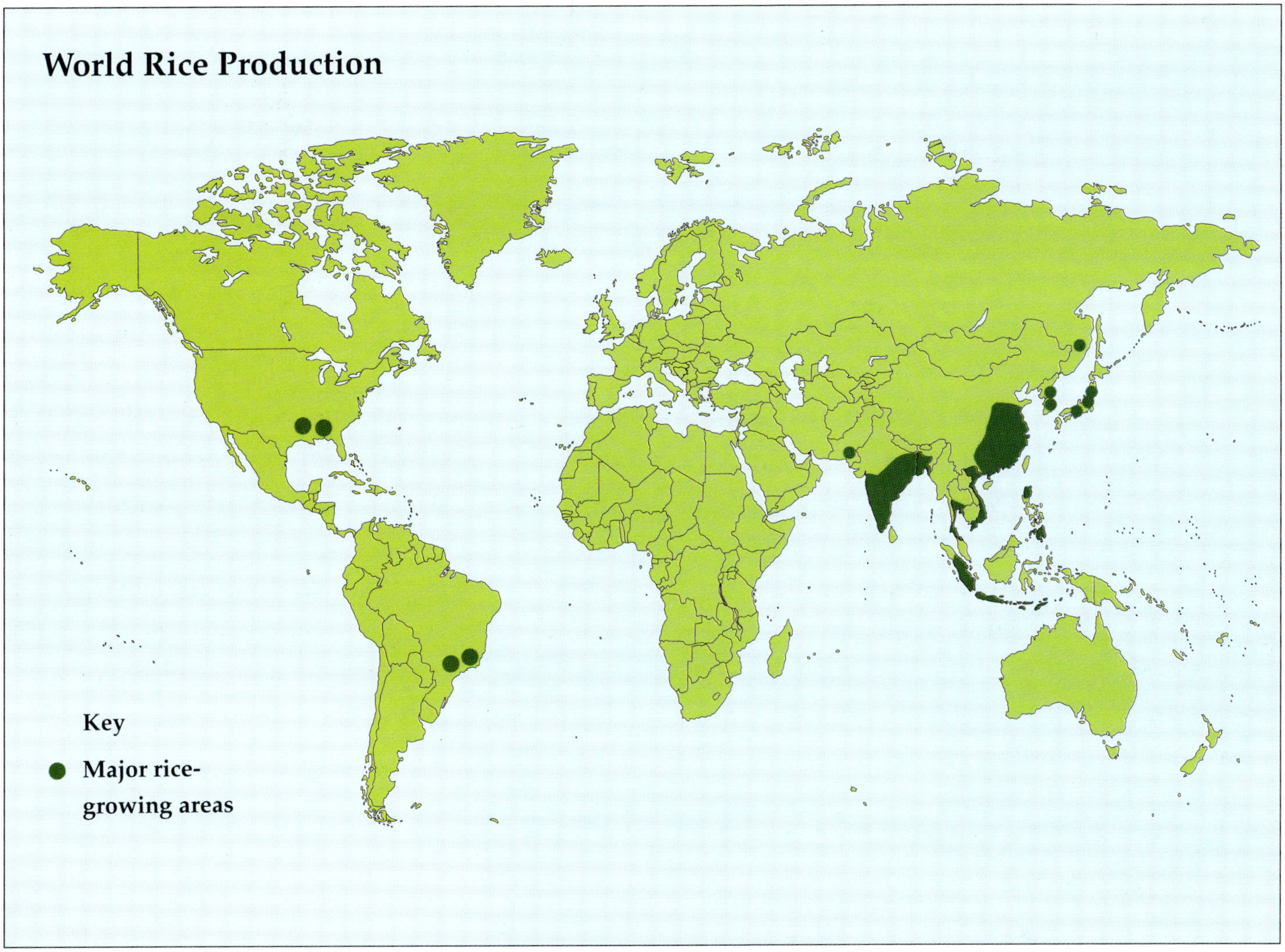

also made on terraced hillsides, creating a fascinating landscape. Most work in paddies is done by hand, although water buffaloes are often used for plowing.

Sorghum and millet

Sorghum and millet are two cereal crops grown in warm climates. In parts of Asia and Africa where they are major food crops, the grain is made into flour. Elsewhere, sorghum and millet are grown mainly to provide food for cattle, in the form of grain, hay, or silage.

Total world sorghum production is more than 64 million tons per year. India grows the most sorghum for food (13 million tons a year). The U.S. grows more (15.5 million tons), but uses it mainly as cattle feed. India also grows the most millet – more than one-third of the annual world production of about 33 million tons a year.

Vegetables

Vegetables are grown as crops throughout the world, in small backyard gardens and in sprawling farmers' fields. The type of crop grown varies widely – it depends largely on the climate. In cooler climates many crops are now raised in greenhouses for part or all of the year. This helps extend the natural growing season and also enables warm-climate crops to be grown.

▲ A wide variety of vegetables is grown throughout the world.

Vegetable goodness

Vegetables should feature in every healthy diet. They provide carbohydrates and protein as well as vitamins and minerals. Potatoes and yams are particularly rich in carbohydrates, and legumes, such as beans, are rich in protein.

Many vegetables, especially leafy ones, also provide roughage, or fiber, in a diet. Fiber has little food value but is important to the body because it keeps the digestive system running smoothly.

▼ Potatoes are grown in gardens and on farms.

In warmer climates

Yams are grown widely in the tropics. In some places, the yam is known as the "king of vegetables." Yams are the swollen roots, or tubers, of a climbing plant. They can get as heavy as 45 pounds. Sweet potatoes are similar to yams, but can grow much farther north than yams. Cassava, or tapioca, is another tropical plant, and its roots are an important food in many African countries. Among legumes, the soybean is the most widely grown. Rich in protein, soybeans are eaten as seeds and also made into oil, flour, soy milk, and tofu. Other tropical vegetables include eggplant, okra, and breadfruit.

In cooler climates

Potatoes, the main vegetable in cooler climates, are the tubers of a plant which originally grew only in South America. Cabbages and other members of the cabbage family, such as brussels sprouts, cauliflower, and broccoli, are the most important leaf vegetables.

Among the many other vegetable crops that thrive in cooler climates are carrots, parsnips, beets, onions, and leeks. Legumes that grow in cool climates include peas, runner beans, kidney beans, and broad beans.

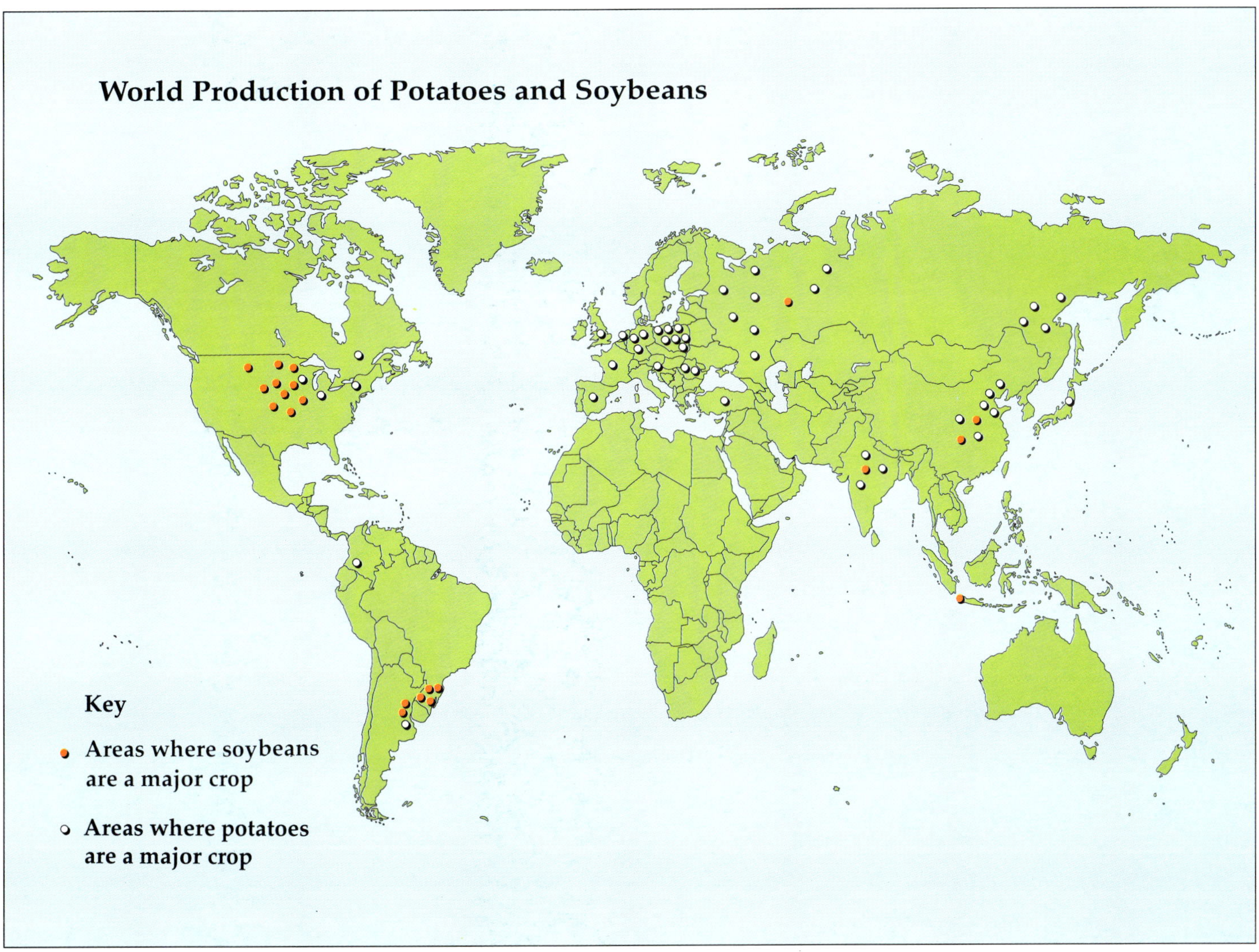

Fruit and Nuts

There is a wide variety of fruits – from the tiny black currant to the watermelon, which can reach more than 88 pounds.

Fruit provides vitamins, minerals, and flavor. Tasty black currants, for example, are rich in vitamin C, and so are oranges.

As with vegetables, the type of fruit grown in any particular region depends on the climate.

▲ Orange trees at harvest time in Chania, Greece.

In warm climates

In the hot and moist climate of tropical and subtropical regions plants grow very quickly and produce large amounts of fruit. Bananas are a popular tropical fruit. They are enjoyed worldwide and form an important part of the diet in Africa, Central and South America, and India.

Date palms flourish in northern Africa and southwest Asia, even in desert conditions. Among the more exotic tropical fruits are pineapple, mango, papaya, guava, and passion fruit.

Citrus fruits – lemons, oranges, and grapefruits – originally from Southeast Asia, are now grown widely. They grow best in climates with hot, dry summers and mild winters. They are grown all over the Mediterranean region. In the U.S., California and Florida are important citrus-growing areas.

The grapevine likes a similar climate and is cultivated all over the Mediterranean, California, Australia, and in many other regions of the world. As well as fresh grapes and raisins (dried grapes), the fruit yields grape juice for winemaking.

In cool climates

Apples are the leading fruit in cool climates, and many varieties are grown. Pears are also popular. Apples and pears grow on trees, as do plums, cherries, and peaches.

Another important group of fruits are berries. Black currants and gooseberries grow on bushes; raspberries and blackberries are climbing plants; and strawberries grow near the ground.

Nuts

Nuts are seeds contained in a hard shell. Among the most popular nuts grown in cooler climates are hazelnuts, almonds, and walnuts. In warmer climates, Brazil nuts and cashews thrive.

The peanut, or ground nut, is actually a vegetable belonging to the pea family, and is not a nut at all. Peanuts are used as a source of oil and are eaten raw or roasted, in candy, or as peanut butter.

▼ Some nuts are processed to extract their oil. Others are eaten raw.

Tea, Coffee, and Chocolate

Tea and coffee are not really foods, but they are often drunk with meals. Both contain a substance called caffeine, a mild stimulant, or "pick-me-up." Chocolate is actually a food.

Tea is the national drink of England, China, Japan, and Russia. India is the world's top tea-growing country, with an annual production of more than 770,000 tons. China and Sri Lanka are the next largest producers.

Tea production

Tea is made from the dried leaves of the tea plant, which thrives in the hot moist climates of southern and southeast Asia. In the wild, the tea plant grows up to 35 feet tall, but on tea plantations it is grown as a shrub that is about the same height as a person.

▼ Workers pick tea leaves on a plantation in southern India.

▲ This crowd of Indonesian coffee workers is sorting the plant's berries.

Leaves are picked by hand from the plant at regular intervals, sometimes once a month. The finest tea is made from the youngest leaves at the tips of the branches. The leaves are picked and crushed before being dried in the sun.

Coffee

Coffee is drunk in large quantities all over the world, with people in the U.S. guzzling the most. Brazil, in South America, is by far the main coffee-producer, with about 3.5 million tons a year. This is five times as much as the second biggest coffee-producer, Colombia, in Central America.

Coffee is made from the berries of the coffee bush. Each berry contains two seeds, called beans. After the beans have been separated from the berry, they are dried and roasted. Roasting brings out the aroma and flavor of coffee.

Chocolate

Chocolate is made from cocoa, obtained from the South American cacao tree. Named after the ancient city Xocolatl in South America, where it originated, chocolate is now grown in tropical climates in many parts of the world.

Cocoa is extracted from the beans found inside the tree's large red-brown fruit pods. The Ivory Coast in West Africa is the world's leading producer of cocoa. Other major producers are Brazil and Ghana, which borders the Ivory Coast.

Coffee-Producing Regions in South America

Sugar and Oils

The world uses huge amounts of sugar for sweetening foods and for preserving them, for example, in jam. Most of the world's sugar comes from sugarcane, a plant grown in hot climates. In cooler climates, sugar can be extracted from a root crop called sugar beet.

Sugarcane is a woody grass that grows up to about 13 feet. The stems contain large amounts of sugary sap. Sugarcane is grown throughout the tropical and subtropical parts of the world – in the southern U. S. and Hawaii, Central and South America, the Caribbean, southern Asia, and Australia.

On some sugar plantations the sugarcane is burned just before harvesting. This kills pests, makes the canes easier to handle, and concentrates the juice inside. Workers then cut the cane with large hooked knives. The cut cane is transported by road or rail to sugar mills, where it is crushed to extract the sap.

Plant oils

Sugar plants provide a source of energy in the form of carbohydrates. Other plants contain fats, another source of energy. These fats are obtained from seeds and nuts as oils. Olive oil, which has been used for thousands of years for cooking and for food dressings, is obtained by crushing the fleshy fruit of the olive tree.

▶ Sugar cane being harvested in North Queensland, Australia

Many other vegetable oils are now used in the food industry, not only for cooking but also in manufacturing such products as margarine. Oils obtained from the seeds of sunflowers and the cotton plant, soybeans, and coconuts are now widely used. Vegetable oil is made up of unsaturated fats, which are healthier to eat than animal fats.

▲ Sunflower seeds can be crushed to make sunflower oil.

PART TWO

Raising Livestock

People have been raising animals for their meat, milk, and skins for at least 14,000 years. Sheep were the first animals to be domesticated, followed by goats, cattle, and pigs. Hundreds of millions of these four types of animals are now raised throughout the world.

The most numerous are cattle, with some 1.5 billion worldwide. India has the most cattle, but for religious reasons they are not eaten. Indian cattle are used to provide milk and as draft animals to pull wagons and plows.

After cattle, sheep are the animals most widely raised. More than one billion are kept throughout the world. Australia has by far the biggest sheep population, with over 160 million – about ten times the number of people in Australia.

▶ White cows are sacred to Hindus. This one has been decorated for a festival.

There are about 800 million pigs in the world. Pigs are kept in most countries, but the largest numbers are in Asia. The 450 million or so goats in the world are multipurpose animals. Goats provide milk (which is widely used in the production of cheeses), meat, hair, and hides.

For sheer numbers, however, chickens cannot be beaten. Chickens are raised for their meat and their eggs. Around the world there are more than seven billion chickens, which provide about one-third of all meat consumed. The other main kinds of poultry raised are turkeys, ducks, and geese.

Among other large livestock raised on farms, water buffalo are important, particularly in southern and southeast Asia. They are raised for their meat and milk and also as draft animals. A few herds of water buffalo are raised in other places, such as Australia, Egypt, and Italy. Their milk is used to make cheeses such as the Italian mozzarella.

▶ In many places, livestock are raised in mixed herds. This herd in Sudan includes goats, cows, and camels.

Cattle Farming

In many countries, cattle are the most important livestock. The term cattle includes cows (females), bulls (males), and calves (male and female young). Beef cattle are cows raised mainly for their meat. Dairy cattle are raised mainly for their milk.

Cattle have been domesticated for centuries. During this time, specialist breeds of beef and dairy cattle have been produced by selective breeding (see page 28). They have been bred from bulls and cows specially selected and reared for their ability to produce beef or milk.

Other cattle breeds have been selectively bred to withstand the heat so that they can be raised in warm and hot climates. Known as "zebu" breeds, they are easily recognized. They have a distinctive hump at the shoulders and a narrow head with long, drooping ears.

▲ Cattle are brought together in pens at a cattle market in England.

THE AUROCHS

All domestic breeds of cattle are thought to have descended from the aurochs, or wild ox, of Europe, which is now extinct. This looked like the fierce fighting bulls (left) of present-day Spain, but was much larger. It stood over 6 feet tall at the shoulders and had large, curved horns.

▲ These cattle are being used to draw farm equipment in southern Pakistan.

Cattle ranching

In the United States, Australia, and parts of South America, beef cattle are raised on the open range. The cattle are left to fend for themselves for most of the time, browsing on natural vegetation. Australia has by far the biggest ranches, and Australians call them cattle stations. The Anna Creek cattle station in South Australia covers about 12,000 square miles, which is nearly the size of Belgium.

By contrast, dairy cows are kept close to the farm, because they have to be milked twice a day. Dairy cattle need a nutritious diet if they are to continue giving enough milk. When the grass stops growing in winter, they are fed on grain, hay, silage, and vegetables.

Beef and Dairy Breeds

Beef cattle have been bred to have a broad, sturdy body. Animals called bullocks or steers are raised for beef: these are male cattle that have had their reproductive organs removed. Only a few mature bulls are kept for breeding.

One of the leading beef breeds is the Hereford; this is the famous breed of the American West, where it is ranched in huge numbers. Shorthorn cattle are also popular in the U.S. Both breeds came from England, as did another widespread beef breed, the dark brown Aberdeen Angus.

A popular French breed is the white Charolais, which is very muscular and gains weight quickly. In warm climates, a favored breed is the Brahman, which is a zebu type. The Santa Gertrudis, a cross between the Brahman and the Shorthorn, also fares well in warm climates and is common in the southern U.S.

Dairy breeds

In contrast to beef animals, dairy cattle are bred with a lean body and a wide rib cage. Young female cattle are called heifers before they give birth to a calf, and cows thereafter. Cows have to calve before they can give milk.

On some dairy farms the cows mate naturally with bulls. But on larger farms, cows are fertilized by artificial insemination: sperm is taken from the bull and introduced into the cow artificially. After calving, cows continue to give milk for up to ten months. They produce on average about 12 quarts of milk per day.

The world's leading dairy breeds include the Friesian, Holstein, Brown Swiss, Guernsey, and Jersey.

▼ A hardy Aberdeen Angus. Its long hair protects it from the cold weather in its native Scotland.

Friesians give the most milk: 6,300 quarts or more per year. Guernseys and Jerseys, which came from the Channel Islands of Guernsey and Jersey in the English Channel, give the creamiest milk.

Most of the milk produced by cows is drunk alone or served in other drinks. Large amounts are also made into cream, butter, cheese, and other products.

◀ Milk can be made into a wide variety of cheeses.

Dairy farming in Switzerland

Pigs

Unlike most other livestock, pigs are raised for just one thing – their meat. Pig meat is eaten fresh as pork, and large amounts are also eaten cured, or preserved, as bacon, ham, and salami.

Some people will not eat pig meat. Jews and Muslims are prevented by their religion from doing so. From a farming point of view, however, the pig is a very useful animal. Pigs are very quick breeders. A sow takes about four months to give birth after she has mated with the boar, and she can produce as many as 25 piglets. After feeding them for a month or so, the sow can be mated again.

▲ The American Duroc is a leading breed of pig.

Leading breeds

Many of today's pig breeds are the result of selective breeding. The Large White, for instance, has been mixed with other breeds to produce several new breeds.

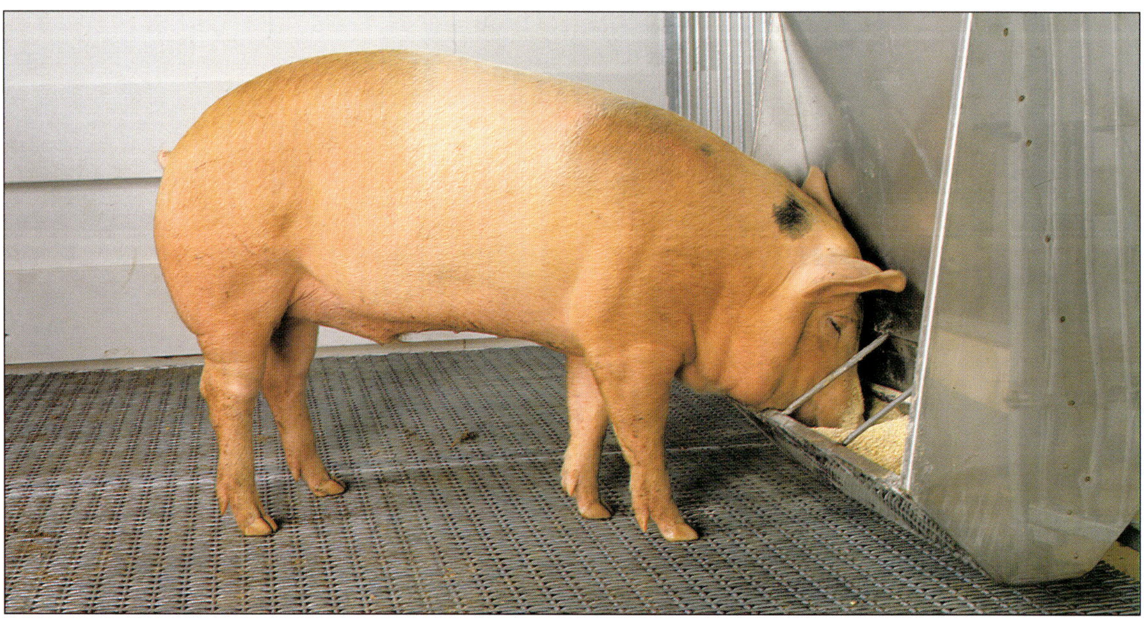

▶ Some farmers use machines that give a premeasured amount of food released by a timer.

Pig Rearing Around the World

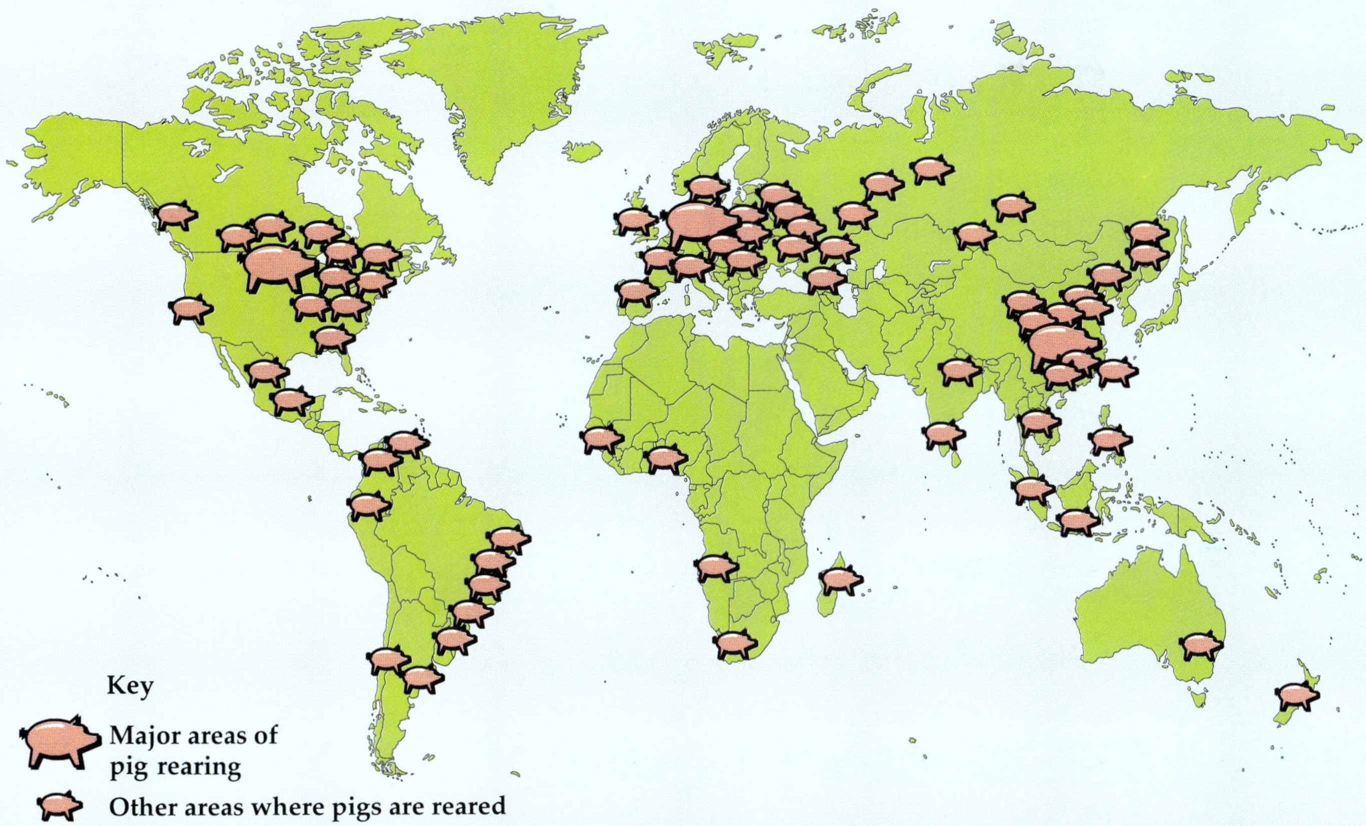

One of the best crosses is with the native Scandinavian pig, the Landrace, giving the Danish Landrace. This is now one of the world's top breeds. In the U.S., the Duroc is a top breed. The Duroc is descended from pigs brought to the New World by Columbus five centuries ago. The Poland China is another American breed, produced from old American stock crossed with animals imported from China.

Raising pigs

In many parts of Asia pigs are raised almost as part of the family, living on household scraps. In other places, pigs are kept on farms in sties, in fields, or in factory farms. Factory-farm pigs are kept in a controlled environment, and they are fed a premeasured amount of food. Under such conditions they fatten very quickly. Many are ready for market when they are about three months old.

Sheep and Goats

Raised in all parts of the world, sheep and goats can forage for food much better than cattle, on rough pasture and other vegetation. Goats browse even on the thorniest of bushes. Goats probably come from the East.

Sheep are raised both for their meat and for their woolly fleece, which is sheared once a year. The meat of mature sheep is called mutton, but mostly it is the meat of young sheep – lambs – that is eaten.

Among sheep breeds, the Merinos are the most popular. They are derived from a Spanish sheep. The Rambouillet is also widely raised, particularly in France and the United States. It was developed in France from a cross between the Merino and the Leicester, an English breed. The New Zealand Corriedale is another important Merino cross-breed.

Sheep are almost always raised on land that is unsuitable for other kinds of farming. Australia has sheep stations covering tens of thousands of acres. Sheep need little tending. For most of the time they roam freely, being rounded up only for lambing, shearing, and treatment with insecticide to control ticks and other pests.

How to tell sheep from goats

Goats look similar to sheep, but there are many differences between them. Goats have a much coarser coat of hair rather than wool. They usually have a beard,

▶ This Sudanese boy milks one of his family's goats.

▲ In New Zealand, sheep stations raise huge numbers of sheep.

and the males (often called billy goats) have a strong smell. Above all, goats have a different temperament. They are lively, inquisitive, and make good pets.

Many breeds of goats have been developed over the centuries in different parts of the world. Two basic types are most widely raised: the Swiss, with its short ears, and the Nubian.

The Nubian, from North Africa, has long, drooping ears.

The Anglo-Nubian, a cross between an English breed and the Nubian, has become a favorite milk breed, and so has the Swiss Saanen. Goat's milk is easier to digest than cow's milk. It is nourishing, and makes excellent cheese and yogurt.

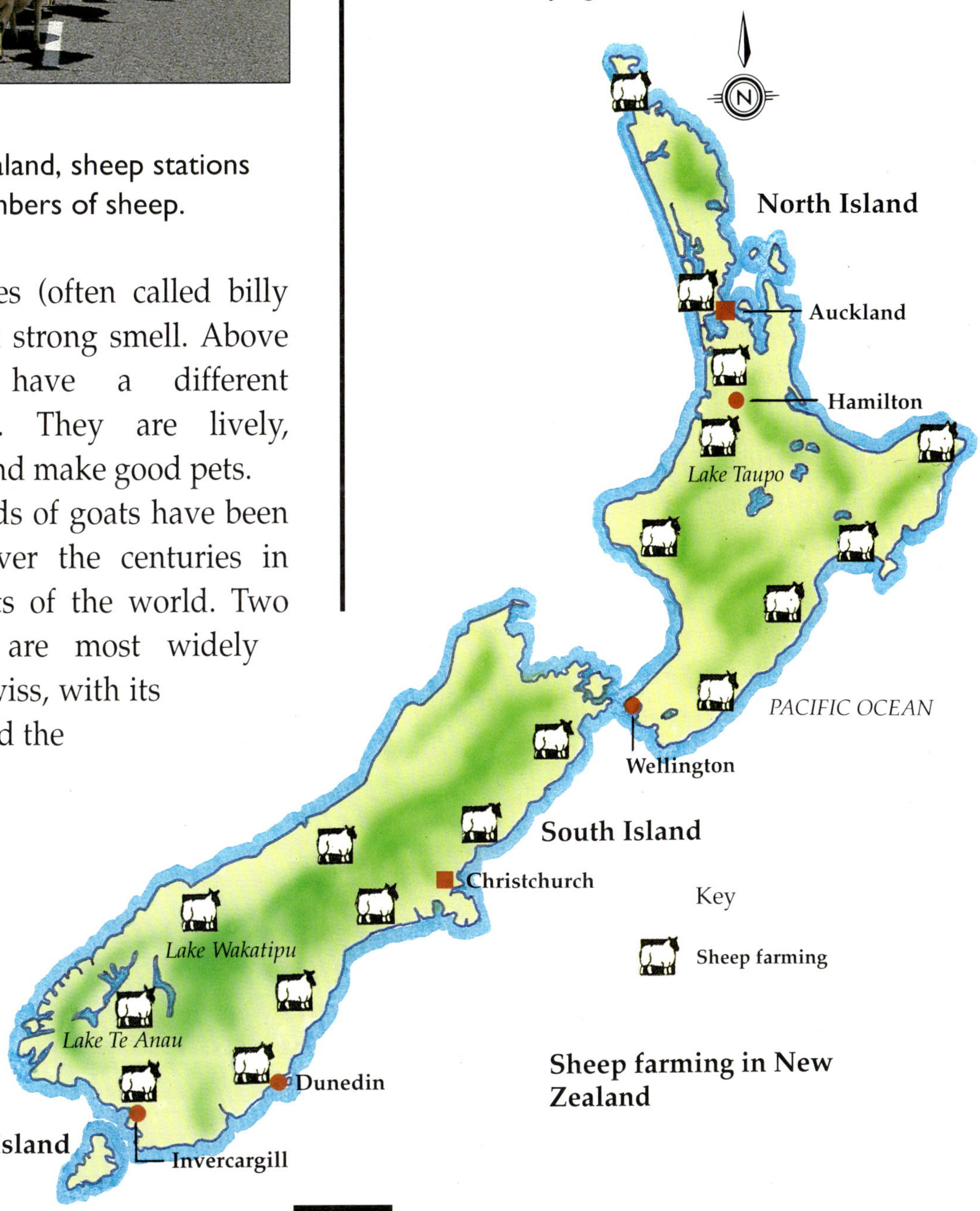

Sheep farming in New Zealand

Chickens

Chickens far outnumber other poultry raised for meat and eggs. They are descended from the jungle fowl of southern Asia.

Basically, chickens are scavengers, feeding on anything they can find – grains, insects, worms, and food scraps. Families throughout the world keep a few chickens for their own use, letting them roam to feed by themselves.

Many small farmers keep larger numbers, feeding them on grain and other food and allowing them to run free for most of the time. These are called free-range birds.

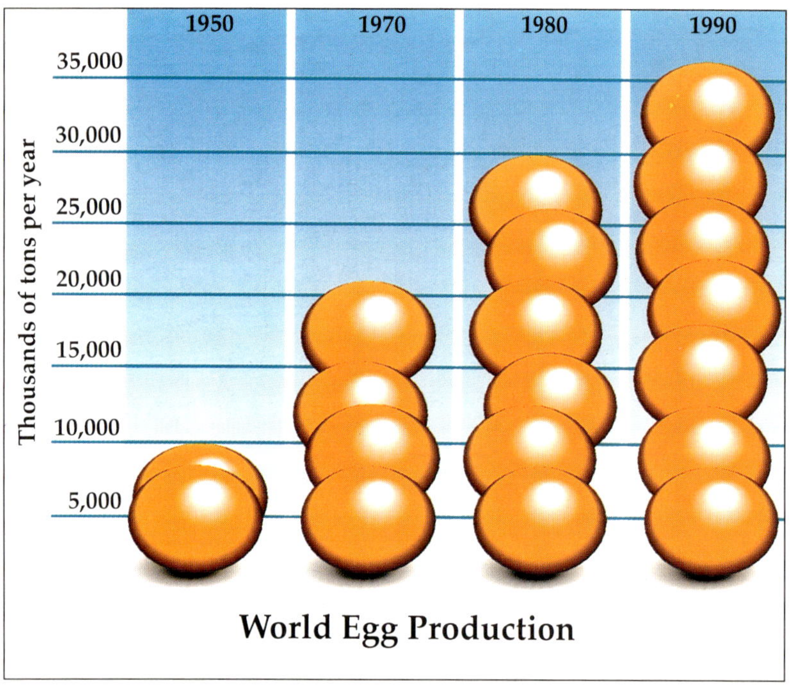

▲ This chart shows that world egg production has risen greatly during the four decades since 1950.

Broilers and battery hens

Most chickens are raised, thousands at a time, on factory farms. The birds are kept inside in controlled conditions and fed a strict diet.

Broilers (chickens that are raised for meat) are ready for the table when they are about eight weeks old, when they weigh about 4.5 pounds. One of the most common meat breeds is a U.S. crossbreed called the Plymouth Rock.

Hens for laying eggs are crammed into tiny cages, called batteries. Their "day" is controlled by switching artificial lighting on and off. This ensures that they lay the maximum number of eggs in a year (about 300). The favored battery hen is the Leghorn, a breed that came from Italy.

Many people dislike this factory-farming approach to raising chickens and consider it to be cruel. Although factory-farmed chicken is cheaper to produce than free-range chicken, some people are prepared to pay more for free-range meat and eggs.

▶ Battery hens remain cramped in cages all their short lives.

PART THREE

Food from the Water

Fish harvested from the sea have been a major source of food since prehistoric times. Fish are rich in protein, oils, vitamins, and minerals.

On average, fish now provide people with about 15 percent of their protein, but the amount of fish eaten varies from country to country. In Japan, for example, fish provide people with about 60 percent of their protein. In many rural areas, particularly in Africa, fish from lakes and rivers are the only regular source of protein.

▲ This Brazilian man fishes from the beach.

On the continental shelves

In total about 90 million tons of fish are caught in the world's oceans each year. Over one-third of the catch is made into fish meal for feeding to animals.

Most fish are caught in the Northern Hemisphere, in the relatively shallow seas above the continental shelf. Nutrients are washed into these seas from the continental rivers and provide food for minute organisms called plankton, on which most fish feed.

▶ This fisherman is unloading the catch from his trawler.

In the Southern Hemisphere there are rich fishing grounds off South America and southwestern Africa where deep water, rich in nutrients, rises to the surface. Plankton, which feed on the nutrients, attract large schools of fish.

Fish species

A great variety of fish species are caught for food. Those caught at sea vary in size, from tiny sprats and sardines a few inches long to swordfish and tuna, which can reach several feet in length.

In terms of quantity, the Alaskan pollack, Japanese and Chilean pilchards, codfish, and Atlantic cod are the most important species. Mackerel, anchovy, herring, whiting, and tuna are also caught in large quantities. In addition to these fish, another important source of food from the sea is shellfish such as shrimps, crabs, lobsters, mussels, clams, and oysters.

Fishing Methods

In many parts of the world, commercial fishermen catch fish using rod, line, and hook in much the same way that anglers do. The fish are attracted to a small piece of bait on the hook.

Some fishermen trail baited hooks behind a boat, which is called long-line fishing. For some fish, such as tuna, the hooks need not even be baited – the fish bite at anything that hangs before them.

Most fish, however, are caught by means of nets. In some countries, fishermen use hand nets and operate close to the shore. But most commercial fishermen cast their nets from boats.

Nets and trawls

One type of net is the drift net. This is a weighted net that hangs vertically down from floats on the surface. Made from synthetic fiber, drift nets are almost invisible to fish, which get caught by their gills in the mesh. Most nets are several miles long; some are up to 30 miles long.

▶ These Sri Lankan fishermen are hauling their net directly onto the beach.

FISH FARMING

Japan and China lead the world in fish farming. This means raising fish in enclosed areas, either in inland ponds or in coastal shallows. Fish farming in eastern Asia dates back centuries. Only recently has it become important elsewhere. Carp, milkfish, and grouper are commonly farmed in Asia; salmon and trout in Europe and the U.S. The picture below shows a trout farm.

The third important netting method is trawling. The trawl is a funnel-shaped net that is dragged through the water at a certain depth, or along the seabed.

In some fishing grounds, factory fishing fleets operate. These fleets are made up of many small fishing boats that pass their catches to a large factory ship. Here the fish are cleaned, processed, and then frozen. The fleet can remain at sea for months at a time.

A purse seine is a net towed in a circle around a school. Cables attached to the net are drawn together, forming a "purse" to catch the fish.

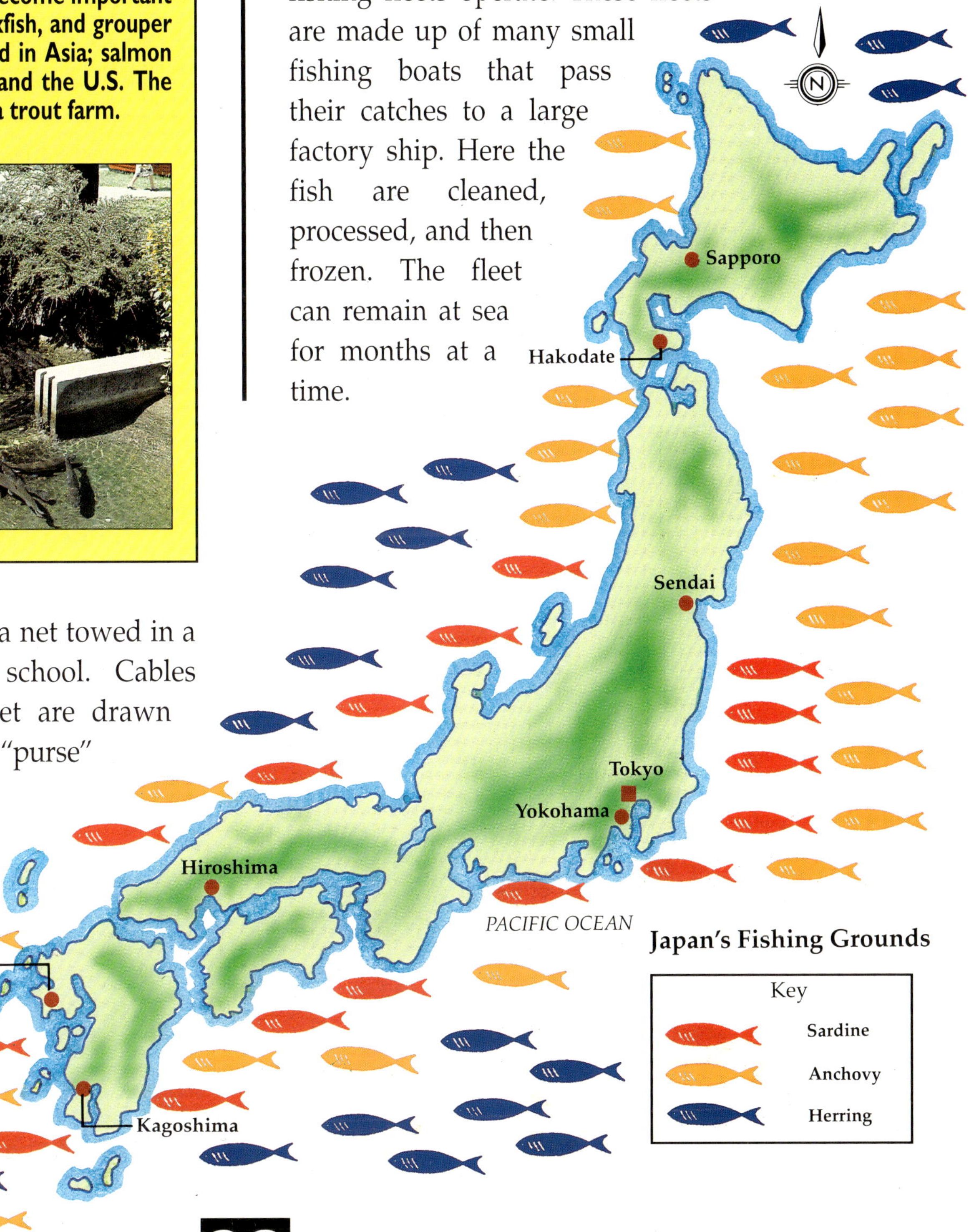

Japan's Fishing Grounds

Losing Land

Modern farming methods have resulted in a huge increase in food production during the last half of this century. However, these methods have created new problems.

Many of these problems are associated with the chemicals farmers use to fertilize the ground and to protect crops from weeds, diseases, and insect pests.

For fertilizer, farmers use chemicals rich in nitrates. However, if they apply too much, rainwater washes the nitrates from the soil and into rivers. The nitrates may find their way into drinking water, making it dangerous to drink.

▼ This farmer is spraying a field with fertilizer. If too much fertilizer is used it can pollute local water supplies.

▲ The water in this canal has been polluted by chemicals originally sprayed onto fields.

Wildlife is also harmed. Nitrates in the rivers cause small water plants to multiply in numbers. As the plants die and rot away, they remove the oxygen from the water. Because of this process, which is called eutrophication, fish and other aquatic animals are unable to live in the water.

The use of chemical herbicides, fungicides, and pesticides can be even more harmful. Some of the latest ones are relatively safe, if used properly, but others contain chemical compounds that are harmful to wildlife. These chemicals get into the food chain, build up in the bodies of animals, and poison them. Some of the deadliest pesticides, such as DDT, are now banned in some countries, but not in others. The pollution danger remains.

Desertification

Vast areas of farmland are being lost each year through soil erosion. This is happening even in developed countries, including the U.S. However, soil erosion has its worst effect in regions with a dry climate, and which appear to be getting even drier.

This process, which is called desertification, is occurring at an alarming rate in Africa. The problem is being made worse by the clearing of trees from the land and by overgrazing by herds of livestock. Goats are especially destructive because they eat most vegetation, even the roots of plants. With nothing left to bind the soil, the land turns to desert.

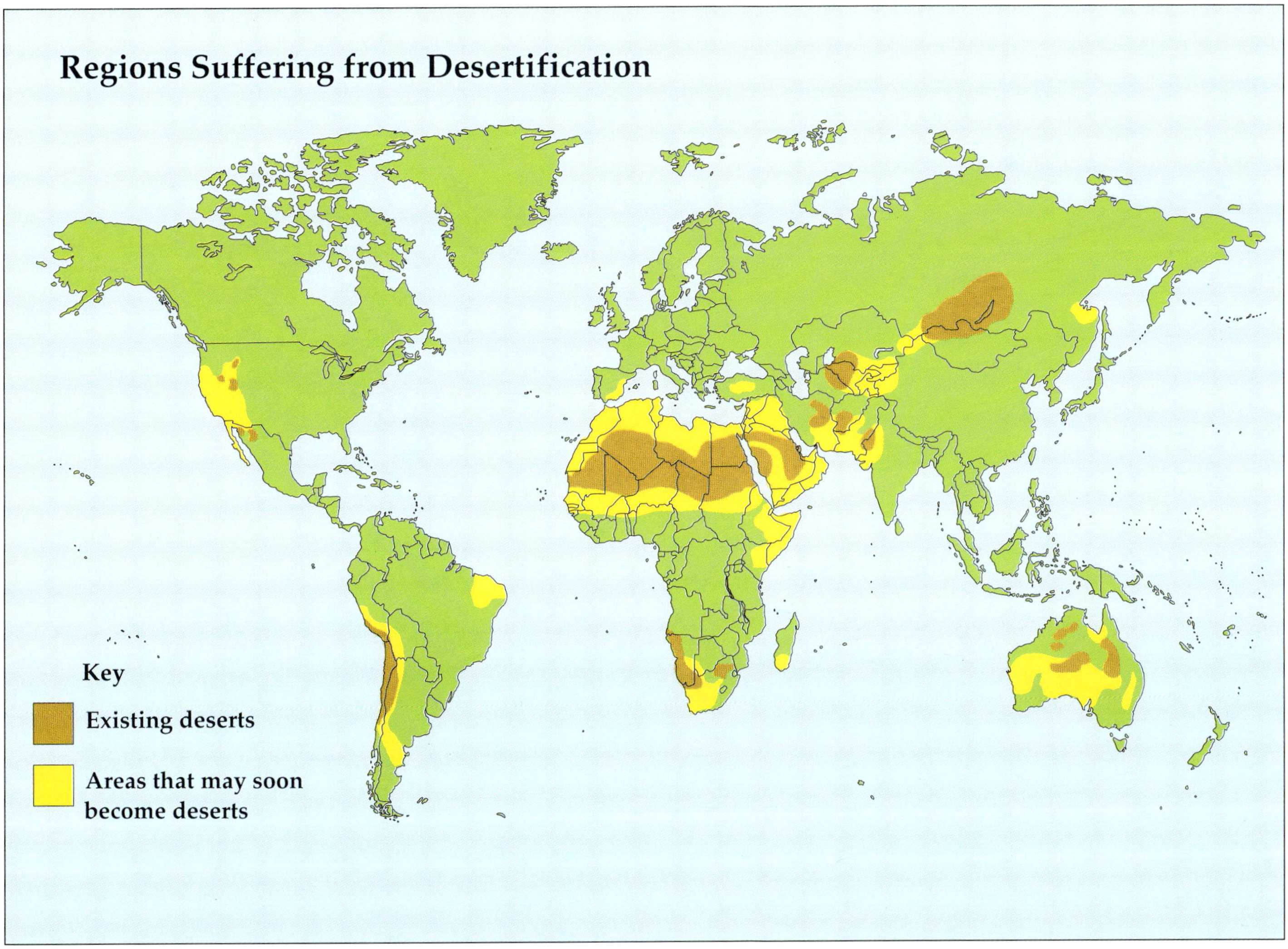

Future Problems

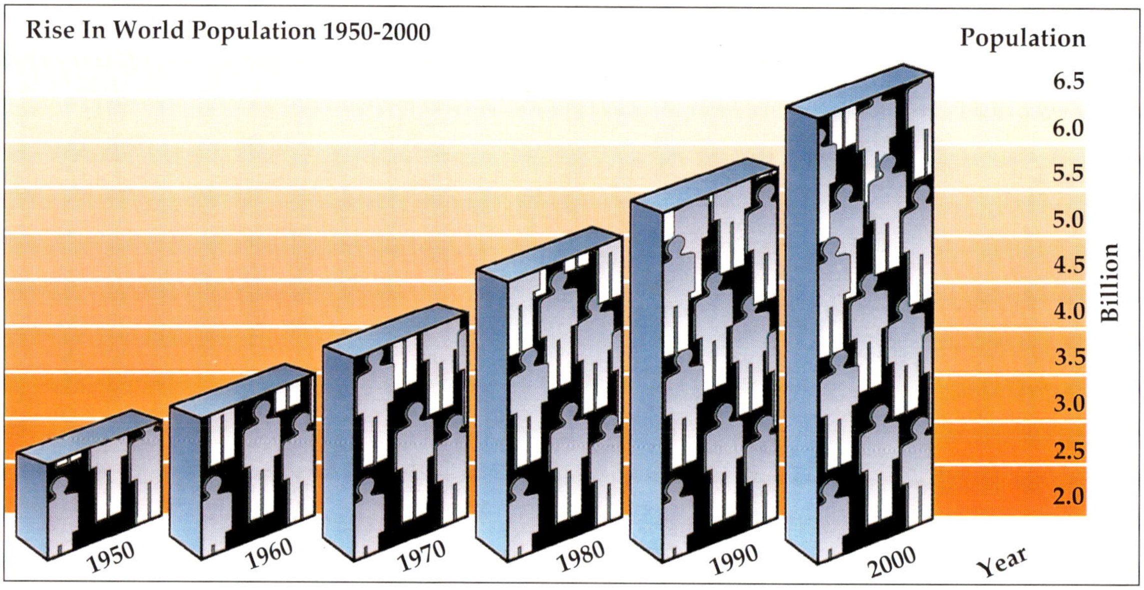

▶ The world's population is predicted to rise to more than six billion in the year 2000.

One of the greatest problems concerning food resources is the world's rapidly increasing population. It is a struggle even now to produce enough food for the present world population of about 5.5 billion people; and every day there are another quarter of a million mouths to feed.

By next century the population of the world could be double what it is now. How are we going to feed 11 billion people?

Better crops

Scientists will certainly help farmers by developing new varieties of grains and other crops. They will use techniques such as genetic engineering to make crops that produce a bigger harvest and that are resistant to disease. For example, scientists should be able to introduce genes into plants so that they "fix" nitrogen, or take it directly from the air. These plants would then be self-fertilizing.

The scientists should also be able to introduce genes that will make plants more resistant to drought. This will become particularly important if desertification begins to accelerate.

Fish famine

People once thought that the oceans were capable of providing an endless supply of fish; but this is not true. The amount of fish caught has declined dramatically in recent years. In the North Sea, for example, catches of herring have dropped from about 4.5 million tons in the mid-1960s to less than one million tons today.

The problem has been caused by modern methods of fishing. Fishing boats use the latest technology, including satellite measurements, to detect schools of fish. They use bigger nets with smaller mesh to catch more fish. So many are caught that the fish population cannot replenish itself each year.

◀ A research unit where scientists produce new breeds of crops

In the future, fishing will have to be carefully regulated by an international agreement to prevent this overfishing. People must learn that the supply of fish in the sea is definitely not endless.

▼ Frozen marlin on sale in a Japanese market. Fishing is one of Japan's major industries.

Future Solutions

One approach to the problems of farming in arid climates will be to introduce new kinds of crop plants that have a natural resistance to drought. For example, there is an Australian grass that produces plenty of grain even in the years when there is little or no rain. Investigating types of drought-resistant plants is just part of the extensive research being carried out to create plants that will grow better in climates where staple crops do not grow well.

New livestock

The livestock farmers in developed countries raise today are the product of centuries of crossbreeding. They are very different from their wild ancestors and in general they are less able to withstand harsh conditions. However, these new breeds are raised because they tend to produce more meat, milk, or wool. In most regions of the world where such new breeds have been introduced, they have succeeded in replacing the native breeds of livestock almost completely.

▶ In recent years, some countries have built enormous dams to provide water for hydroelectric power and for irrigation. However, they are now finding that the traditional small-scale methods (right) may be more successful.

▲ Red deer graze contentedly on a deer farm in Scotland.

Although less productive, native animals are usually better suited to the local climate. Cattle from the colder northern countries, for example, usually have long coats to keep them warm.

Another advantage of native animals is that they can exist by browsing on leaves and branches, as well as by grazing on tough grass. Because of this, some people are now beginning to think that the native animals might make better livestock than imported "farm" animals. In some parts of the world this theory is already being tested. In East Africa, for example, native wild breeds such as kudu and eland are now being raised. In New Zealand, the beautiful red deer are becoming important as commercial livestock.

Deer are also being raised in Scotland and elsewhere in northern Europe. In the cold far north, moose could be a familiar source of meat in the future.

Carbohydrate A substance that contains carbon, hydrogen, and oxygen. Carbohydrates are an important food group. Bread, potatoes, sugar, and pasta contain large amounts of carbohydrates.

Cultivation All the stages that are necessary for producing crops, including preparing the land, sowing seeds, tending the crops as they grow, and harvesting them.

Digestive system The group of bodily organs that enable an animal to take in food and turn it into substances that the body can use.

Domesticate To tame a wild animal, often so that it can be used for its produce.

Factory farming A system of farming that makes use of many of the methods used in a factory. For instance, animals may be kept in pens, under artificial lights on a timer, and fed automatically by machine.

Fats Substances produced by animals and some plants. Fats supply the body with energy.

Fertilizer A substance that is used to help plants grow. Fertilizers can be artificial (made with chemicals) or natural. Animal dung and compost (rotting plant material) are natural fertilizers.

Fiber Another word for roughage.

Food chain A chain of plants and animals that are linked together: an animal eats a plant and is in turn eaten by a larger animal, which is eaten by an even larger animal, and so on.

Fungicide A chemical that kills a fungus. Some crops are sprayed with a fungicide to protect them from diseases caused by fungi.

Genes A code in every cell of every plant and animal. Genes determine physical characteristics, such as hair and eye color.

Genetic engineering The scientific process of altering the genes of a plant or animal to improve the species.

Herbicide A substance that kills plants, particularly weeds that could stunt the growth of crops.

Insecticide A substance that kills insects that might harm crops or livestock.

Legume Any plant that grows seeds in a pod. Peas and beans are legumes.

Mineral A chemical substance that is inorganic (not living). Minerals in very tiny amounts are necessary for a healthy body. Minerals include iron and calcium.

Nitrate A chemical compound containing nitrogen. It is found naturally in soil, but is also added to the soil in fertilizers.

Nitrogen The main gas found in air. This element is vital for plant growth.

Pesticide A substance that kills any pest, including insects, fungi, and weeds.

Phosphate A substance containing phosphorus that is naturally present in some rocks and in animal and plant remains. Phosphates are necessary for plant growth and are added to soil in fertilizers.

Prairie A type of landscape with flat or rolling land, low-growing plants, and few trees. There are prairies in central North America.

Protein A substance that is made up of carbon, hydrogen, oxygen, and nitrogen. Protein is an important nutrient, providing the building blocks for growth. Foods containing protein include meat, cheese, milk, and eggs.

Roughage The "rough" parts of some foods that helps the digestive system to run smoothly. It is found in foods such as bran, and in some fruits and some vegetables.

Selective breeding A method of breeding animals that have desirable characteristics, such as growing very quickly. Individual animals are selected because they have these characteristics, and they are used to produce young. Individuals that do not have the characteristics are not selected for breeding.

Silage Food for animals that is storied in a silo, where it ferments.

Soil erosion Loss of fertile soil from the land. Soil erosion can be caused by a number of practices, including intensive farming and overgrazing.

Sperm A male cell that fertilizes a female egg cell to produce a baby.

Staple A basic food that is eaten at almost all meals.

Steppe A type of landscape, similar to a prairie, that is flat and has low vegetation and few trees. Steppes are found mainly in eastern Europe and Asia, especially in the former Soviet Union.

Subtropical climate A climate like that of the southeastern part of the United States, with hot summers, mild winters, and rain all year round.

Temperate climate A climate that has neither extremes of heat nor extremes of cold. Areas with a temperate climate include the northwestern coast of the United States and the British Isles.

Tropical climate The kind of climate found in the tropics. The weather there is generally very hot with torrential storms.

Tropics The region of the world that lies on either side of the equator, between the Tropic of Cancer to the north and the Tropic of Capricorn to the south.

Tuber A plant with a thickened root from which new plants grow. The potato is an edible tuber.

Vitamin One of a number of food substances essential for health.

Further Reading

Agribusiness. Irving, TX: Boy Scouts of America, 1987.

Chrisp, Peter. *The Farmer Through History*. Journey Through History. New York: Thomson Learning, 1993.

Dineen, Jacqueline. *Food from Dairy and Farmyard.* Hillside, NJ: Enslow Publishers, 1988.

Gibb, Christopher. *Food or Famine.* Vero Beach, FL: Rourke Corp, 1987.

Lambert, Mark. *Farming Technology*. New York: Franklin Watts, 1990.

Reed-King, Susan. *Food and Farming*. Young Geographer. New York: Thomson Learning, 1993.

Smith, David. *The Food Cycle*. Natural Cycles. New York: Thomson Learning, 1993.

Swallow, Su. *Food for the World*. Austin: Raintree Steck-Vaughn, 1991.

Picture Acknowledgments

The publishers would like to thank the following for supplying photographs: J. Allan Cash Library: cover, pages 8 bottom, 12 top, 18, 23, 36, 38, 39, 40 top and bottom, 43, and 45; Hutchison Picture Library: pages 8 top, 24, 25, 32, and 42; Wayland Picture Library: cover, pages 5, 6, 10, 12 bottom, 14, 16 top and bottom, 20 top and bottom, 22, 26 top, 27, 28, 29, and 33; Zefa: cover, pages 19, 26 bottom, 30 top and bottom, 35, and 44.

INDEX

Page numbers in **bold** refer to pictures and text. Others refer only to text.